CHARLES CAMILLE SAINT-S NS

LE CAR
AN
DER KARN IERE

Grande Fant ogique

Edited by/Hera gegeben von

Felix Aprahamian

Ernst Eulenburg Ltd

London · Mainz · New York · Paris · Tokyo · Zürich

Ernst Eulenburg Ltd, 48 Great Marlborough Street,
London W1V 2BN

C. SAINT–SAËNS

The Carnival of Animals

Humour in music, apart from the musical setting of a humorous text, is a phenomenon much more rarely encountered than might be supposed. The musical accompaniment of even a comic poem may be intrinsically unfunny. Wordless music which provokes merriment does this by parody, quotation, with or without distortion, or by tonal descriptiveness. In *Le Carnaval des Animaux,* Camille Saint-Saëns left a rare example of musical humour which includes all this. It has a curious and fascinating history and presents the probably unique example of a work withdrawn by its composer after a few performances – save for one excerpt which gained worldwide popularity – and then published posthumously under the terms of his will.

It is, perhaps, ironic that *Le Cygne,* the piece by which Saint-Saëns, a composer of operas, symphonies, concertos and the like, is best known, comes from a work which he never allowed to be published complete in his lifetime. *Le Cygne* was published in 1887, a year after its composition, but *Le Carnaval des Animaux,* of which it forms a part, remained in manuscript until much later. When Saint-Saëns died in 1921 at the age of eighty-six and very much the doyen of French music at the time, his will was found to contain the following clause about his manuscripts:

> I expressly forbid the publication of any unpublished work, except *Le Carnaval des Animaux,* which may be issued by my usual publishers, MM. Durand et Cie.

So, thirty-five years after they were written, these fourteen pieces, making up what their composer sub-titled a *Grande Fantaisie Zoölogique,* were issued as a complete work for the first time. Since then, *Le Carnaval des Animaux* has never failed to amuse and divert when two pianos and a handful of instruments – flute, clarinet, glass harmonica (or substitute – never a Harmonica or mouth-organ), xylophone and celesta – have been gathered together.

If *Le Carnaval des Animaux* may now be enjoyed as a musical relaxation, that is just what its composing allowed Saint-Saëns in February 1886. In the previous year, he had published his *Harmonie et Mélodie* – not, as such a title would suggest, a textbook, but a collection of critical writings. The lip-service he paid Wagner's genius in this book left no doubt that his own musical tenets were far removed from those of Bayreuth. At a time when, even in France, Wagnerism had assumed the proportions of a cultural religion, Saint-Saëns's Gallic scepticism and reactionary, academic attitude made him a butt for critical jibes. Neither the book nor its Parisian reviews passed unnoticed in Germany, where Saint-Saëns had become well-known, so that when he toured several German towns as pianist and composer in January, 1886, he met with much hostility, both from the press and from a section of the public incited by it. Although a friendly reception in some places compensated for this, Saint-Saëns's French biographer, Bonnerot, says that it was 'as much to forget this affront as to rest from the tour' that Saint-Saëns withdrew to a small Austrian town and there wrote *Le Carnaval des Animaux,* which lack of time had formerly prevented him from writing for his pupils at the Ecole Niedermeyer, as he had intended to, when he taught the piano there between 1861 and 1865. In 1886 his piano-teaching days were over, and the occasion for which he wrote *Le Carnaval* was the annual Shrove Tuesday concert of a then well-known cellist, Charles Joseph Lebouc, son-in-law of the even better-known tenor, Adolphe Nourrit. *Le Carnaval des Animaux* was first performed *chez Lebouc* on 9 March, 1886, when Louis Diémer and Saint-Saëns himself were the pianists. A few days later, it was repeated at the Lenten concert of *La Trompette,* a select Parisian chamber music society of the time, for which Saint-Saëns had already composed his Septet, Op.46, in 1881. Later in 1886 his friend Liszt visited Paris and, hearing about *Le Carnaval,* requested a performance. This was arranged for him at the home of Madame Viardot. *Le Carnaval des Animaux* was given subsequently on a few special occasions, but it remained in manuscript until Saint-Saëns's will raised his interdict on its publication.

The following tunes are quoted or parodied during the *Carnival:*

Tortues 'La, la, la, la, la, partons, marchons' and 'Ce bal est original, d'un galop infernal' from *Orpheus in the Underworld* by Offenbach.

L'Eléphant The *Danse des Sylphes* from *The Damnation of Faust* by Berlioz; also a hint of the Scherzo from the music for *A Midsummer Night's Dream* by Mendelssohn.

Fossiles The *Danse macabre* by Saint-Saëns himself followed by 'J'ai du bon tabac', 'Ah! vous dirai-je maman'. 'Partant pour la Syrie', and Rosina's Air from *The Barber of Seville* by Rossini.

Felix Aprahamian, 1981

C. SAINT–SAËNS

Le Carnaval des Animaux

En dehors de la mise en musique d'un texte comique, la drôlerie dans la musique est un phénomène que l'on rencontre plus rarement qu'on pourrait le supposer. Même l'accompagnement musical d'un poème comique peut être dépourvu d'une intrinsèque expression comique. La musique sans paroles qui provoque l'hilarité y réussit au moyen de la parodie, la citation (avec ou sans distorsion) ou bien la descriptivité tonale. Dans *Le Carnaval des Animaux,* Camille Saint-Saëns laissa un rare exemple de drôlerie musicale qui comprend tout cela. Cet ouvrage a une histoire curieuse et passionnante et présente l'exemple, probablement unique, d'un ouvrage retiré par son compositeur après quelques exécutions (sauf un morceau, qui gagna une popularité mondiale) et ensuite publié après la mort de l'auteur en conformité des conditions de son testament.

Il est peut-être ironique que *Le Cygne,* le morceau par lequel Saint-Saëns – compositeur d'opéras, de symphonies, de concertos et d'autres oeuvres semblables – est mieux connu, fasse partie d'une oeuvre dont il ne permit jamais la parution complète de son vivant. *Le Cygne* parut en 1887, un an après sa composition, mais *La Carnaval des Animaux,* dont il fait partie, ne fut publié que bien plus tard. Lorsque Saint-Saëns mourut en 1921 á l'âge de quatre-vingt-six ans – à un moment où il était indiscutablement le doyen de la musique française – son testament se révéla contenir la disposition suivante à propos de ses manuscrits:

> Je défends expressément la publication de tout ouvrage inédit, à l'exception du *Carnaval des Animaux,* qui pourra être publié par mes éditeurs habituels, MM. Durand et Cie.

Ainsi, trente-cinque années après leur composition, ces quatorze morceaux qui composent ce que leur compositeur sous-titra *Grande Fantaisie Zoölogique,* parurent pour la première fois en tant qu'une oeuvre complète. Depuis lors, *Le Carnaval des Animaux* n'a jamais manqué d'amuser et de divertir quand deux pianos et un petit nombre d'instruments ont été rassemblés: flûte, clarinette, harmonica, xylophone et célesta.

Si l'on peut maintenant jouir du *Carnaval des Animaux* comme un divertissement musical, sa composition permit effectivement -a Saint-Saëns de se délasser pendant le mois de février, 1886. L'an précédant il avait fait éditer son *Harmonie et Mélodie,* qui n'est pas, comme un tel titre pourrait suggérer, un livre de texte, mais un recueil d'écrits critiques. Les hommages peu sincères qu'il rendit au génie de Wagner dans ce livre ne laissa pas de doute que ses propres principes fûssent bien éloignés de ceux du maître de Bayreuth. A un moment où, même en France, le wagnérisme s'était attribué les proportions d'un culte culturel, scepticisme gallois de Saint-Saëns et son attitude réactionnaire et académique en firent l'objet de moquerie de la part des critiques. Ni le livre nk les comptes rendus parisiens ne passèrent inaperçus en Allemagne, où Saint-Saëns était devenu bien connu, de sorte que quand il fit une tournée en plusieurs villes allemandes en tant que pianiste et compositeur en janvier 1886, il fut accueilli avec beaucoup d'animosité, de la part de la presse aussi bien qu'une section du public, qui avait été montée par les journalistes. Bien que l'accueil favorable en quelques lieux compensât cela, Bonnerot, le biographe français de Saint-Saëns, dit que c'était 'autant pour oublier cet affront que pour se reposer de cette tournée' que Saint-Saëns se retira dans une petite ville autrichienne et y écrivit *Le Carnaval des Animaux*. En effet, le manque de temps l'avait empêché de l'écrire pour ses élèves à l'Ecole Niedermeyer, comme il avait eu l'intention de faire lorsqu'il enseigna le piano là entre 1861 et 1865. En 1886, sa carrière comme professeur de piano était finie, et l'occasion pour laquelle il écrivit *Le Carnaval* fut le concert annuel de Mardi Gras d'un violoncelliste alors bien connu, Charles Joseph Lebouc, gendre du ténor encore mieux connu, Adolphe Nourrit. Lebouc et sa femme cantatrice étaient actifs dans la vie musicale parisienne des années au milieu du siècle dernier, en tant qu'exécutants et professeurs, et avant 1880 ils avaient arrangé pendant plus de vingt années une série annuelle de douze concerts à Paris chaque hiver. La première exécution du *Carnaval des Animaux* eut lieu chez Lebouc le 9 mars 1886; Louis Diémer et Saint-Saëns lui-même furent alors les pianistes. Quelques jours plus tard, il fut répété au concert de Mi-Carême de *La Trompette*, une société musicale parisienne choisie de l'époque, pour laquelle Saint-Saëns avait déjà composé son *Septuor* Op.46 en 1881. Plus tard en 1886, son ami Liszt visita Paris et, entendant parler du *Carnaval*, en demanda une exécution. Celle-ci fut organisée pour lui à la maison de Madame Viardot. Par la suite, le *Carnaval des Animaux* fut donné à quelques reprises spéciales, mais il resta écrit à la main jusqu'au moment où le testament de Saint-Saëns leva l'interdiction de sa publication.

Les mélodies suivantes sont citées ou parodiées au cours du 'carnaval':

Tortues 'La, la la, la, la, partons, marchons' et 'Ce bal est original, d'un galop infernal' d'*Orphée aux enfers* d'Offenbach.

L'Eléphant La *Danse des sylphes* de *La Damnation de Faust* de Berlioz; ainsi q'un écho du Scherzo de la musique pour *Un songe d'une nuit d'été* de Mendelssohn.

Fossiles La *Danse macabre* par Saint-Saëns lui-même, suivie de 'J'ai du bon tabac', 'Ah! vous dirai-je maman', 'Partant pour la Syrie', et l'Air de Rosina du *Barbier de Séville* de Rossini.

Felix Aprahamian, 1981
Traduction française de Freda Pitt

C. SAINT-SAËNS

Der Karneval der Tiere

Humor in der Musik, von Vertonungen humoristischer Texte abgesehen, kommt seltener vor als man annehmen möchte. Selbst Vertonungen komischer Gedichte können völlig humorlos sein. Musik ohne unterlegten Text, die lustig wirkt, erreicht dies durch Parodie, Zitate, die tongetreu übernommen oder verfremdet werden können, oder durch Tonmalerei. Camille Saint-Saëns hat uns in seinem *Carnaval des Animaux* eines der seltenen Beispiele hinterlassen, in dem dies alles auftritt. Das Werk hat eine seltsame und faszinierende Geschichte und ist wahrscheinlich das einzige, das von seinem Komponisten nach einigen Aufführungen zurückgezogen wurde – ein Stück daraus ausgenommen, das in der ganzen Welt populär geworden ist – und das dann nach seinem Tode, laut seiner eigenen testamentarischen Verfügung schließlich doch veröffentlicht wurde.

Es ist in gewissem Sinne eine Ironie des Schicksals, daß *Le Cygne,* das bekannteste Stück von Saint-Saëns, der Opern, Sinfonien, Konzerte und dergleichen komponierte, aus einem Werk stammt, für das er so lange er lebte, nie die Erlaubnis zu einer vollständigen Veröffentlichung gegeben hat. *Le Cygne* erschien 1887, ein Jahr nach der Entstehung des Stücks, der *Carnaval des Animaux* dagegen, zu dem es gehört, blieb noch lange unveröffentlicht. Als Saint-Saëns 1921 im Alter von sechsundachtzig Jahren starb, zu einer Zeit als er durchaus als Doyen der französischen Musik galt, fand sich die folgende, seine Manuskripte betreffenden Klausel in seinem Testament:

> Ich verbiete ausdrücklich die Veröffentlichung aller ungedruckten Werke, mit Ausnahme des *Carnaval des Animaux,* der bei meinem üblichen Verleger, MM. Durand et Cie., erscheinen mag.

So kam es dann, daß diese vierzehn Stücke, denen der Komponist den Untertitel *Grande Fantaisie Zoölogique* gab, erst fünfunddreißig Jahre nach ihrer Entstehung als ein vollständiges Werk herausgegeben wurden. Seither hat der *Carnaval des Animaux* stets für Erheiterung und Unterhaltung gesorgt, wenn immer zwei Klaviere und eine Anzahl von weiteren Instrumenten – Flöte, Klarinette, Glasharmonika (oder ein Ersatzinstrument dafür), Xylophon und Celesta – sich zusammenfanden.

Wenn man sich jetzt des *Carnaval des Animaux* als einer entspannenden musikalischen Unterhaltung erfreuen kann, so ist diese Wirkung genau das, was die Komposition dieses Werks Saint-Saëns selbst im Februar 1886 verschaffte. Im Jahr davor hatte er seine *Harmonie et Mélodie* veröffentlicht, was nicht, wie ein solcher Titel es anzudeuten scheint, ein Lehrbuch, sondern eine Sammlung kritischer Schriften ist. Das Lippenbekenntnis, das er Wagners Genius in diesem Buch zollte, ließ darüber keinen Zweifel, daß sein eigenes musikalisches Bekenntnis von dem Bayreuths weit entfernt war. Zu einer Zeit, in der der Wagnerkult selbst in Frankreich das Ausmaß einer Kulturreligion angenommen hatte, wurde Saint-Saëns durch seinen typisch französischen Skeptizismus und seine reaktionäre, akademische Haltung zum Gegenstand kritischen Spotts. Weder das Buch selbst, noch die darüber in Paris erschienenen Kritiken blieben in Deutschland, wo Saint-Saëns recht bekannt geworden war, unbemerkt, so daß er, als er mehrere deutsche Städte als Pianist und Komponist im Januar 1886 besuchte, von der Presse und von einem Teil der von ihr beeinflußten Bevölkerung oft angefeindet wurde. Wenn ihn auch eine freundliche Aufnahme an einigen Orten dafür entschädigte, war es doch, wie Saint-Saëns' französischer Biograph Bonnerot feststellt, ‚nicht nur, um von der Tournee auszuruhen, sondern ebenso um diesen Affront zu vergessen', daß er sich in eine kleine österreichische Stadt zurückzog, wo er den *Carnaval des Animaux* schrieb. Zeitmangel hatte ihn früher gehindert, das Werk wie er es vorgehabt hatte, für seine Schüler an der Ecole Niedermeyer zu schreiben, als er dort von 1861 bis 1865 Klavierunterricht gab. Die Zeit seiner Tätigkeit als Klavierlehrer war im Jahre 1886 vorüber, und die Gelegenheit, für die er den *Carnaval* schrieb, war ein Konzert, das der damals bekannte Cellist Charles Joseph Lebouc, Schwiegersohn des noch bekannteren Tenors Adolphe Nourrit, alljährlich am Fastnachts—Dienstag gab. Erstmalig wurde der *Carnaval des Animaux* am 9. März 1886 *chez Lebouc,* mit Saint-Saëns und Louis Diémer als Pianisten, aufgeführt. Einige Tage später, in der Fastenzeit, wurde das Werk im Rahmen eines Konzerts der damals exklusiven Kammermusikgesellschaft *La Trompette* wiederholt. Für diese Gesellschaft hatte Saint-Saëns schon 1881 sein Septett Op.46 komponiert. Im weiteren Verlauf des Jahres 1886 besuchte sein Freund Liszt Paris, und als er vom *Carnaval* hörte, bat er um eine Aufführung, die dann für ihn im Haus von Madame Viardot veranstaltet wurde. Danach wurde der *Carnaval des Animaux* noch einige Male bei besonderen Gelegenheiten gespielt, blieb aber Manuskript, bis Saint-Saëns' Testament das Verbot der Veröffentlichung dieses Werks aufhob.

Die folgenden Themen werden im *Carnaval* zitiert oder parodiert:

Tortues ‚La, la, la, la, la, partons, marchons', und ‚Ce bal est original, d'un galop infernal' aus *Orpheus in der Unterwelt* von Offenbach.

L'Elephant *Danse des sylphes* aus *Fausts Verdammung* von Berlioz: außerdem eine Anspielung auf das Scherzo aus Mendelssohns Musik zum *Sommernachtstraum.*

Fossiles Saint-Saëns' eigener *Danse macabre* und danach ‚J'ai du bon tabac', ‚Ah! vous dirai-je maman', ‚Partant pour la Syrie', und Rosinas Arie aus Rossinis *Barbier von Sevilla.*

Felix Aprahamian, 1981
Deutsche Übersetzung Stefan de Haan

Textual Notes

This edition is based on the autograph (AUT) full score in the Bibliothèque Nationale, Paris (MS 2456). A collation of the original with the posthumous first edition (DUR) published by Durand et Cie. reveals the following minor differences:

No.1 b11: AUT has 8va above first seven quavers in Pno II – an obvious omission

No.5 bb21-28: *mf* Cb entry notated an octave lower in AUT

No.7 DUR shows Harm above Fl on stave: the present edition has Fl above Harm as in AUT

No.8 AUT gives *Ad lib:* DUR gives *Tempo ad lib.*

No.9 b36: AUT has obviously erroneous A natural as last lowest crotchet

No.12 b18: DUR shows staccato quavers on beat 2 in Pno I(F,G) and beat 4 in Pno II (E♭,F); staccs not in AUT

b24: AUT shows

producing hidden octaves in outer parts. The editorial alteration (DUR) is retained in the present edition.

Felix Aprahamian

Instruments

Flute (doubling Piccolo)
Clarinet (B♭ & C)
Glass Harmonica
Xylophone
2 Pianos
Strings

LE CARNAVAL DES ANIMAUX

GRAND FANTAISIE ZOÖLOGIQUE

No. 1

Introduction
et Marche royale du Lion

C. Saint-Saëns
1835-1921

No. 1370

E E 6668

Edited by Felix Aprahamian

11
Pft. I
Pft. II
Vl.
I
II
Vla.
Vc.
Cb.
13
2
Allegro non troppo

18
Più allegro
3
Pft. I
Pft. II
I
Vl.
II
Vla.
Vc.
Cb.
ff
24

29
4
Pft.I
Pft.II
1
Vl.
II
Vla.
Vc.
Cb.
34
5
f
ff
pizz.

39
Pft. I
Pft. II
ff
arco
I
Vl.
II
Vla.
Vc.
Cb.
44
6
pizz.

50
Pft. I
p
Pft. II
Vl. I
Vl. II
Vla.
Vc.
Cb.
f
55
7
cresc.
ff

60
8
Pft. I
Pft. II
I
Vl.
II
Vla.
Vc.
Cb.
ff
67
f

No. 2 Poules et Coqs

Cl. (B♭)
Vl. I
Vl. II
Vla.
2
en traînant
en traînant
animato
3
Pft.I
Pft.II

No. 3

Hémiones

(Animaux véloces)

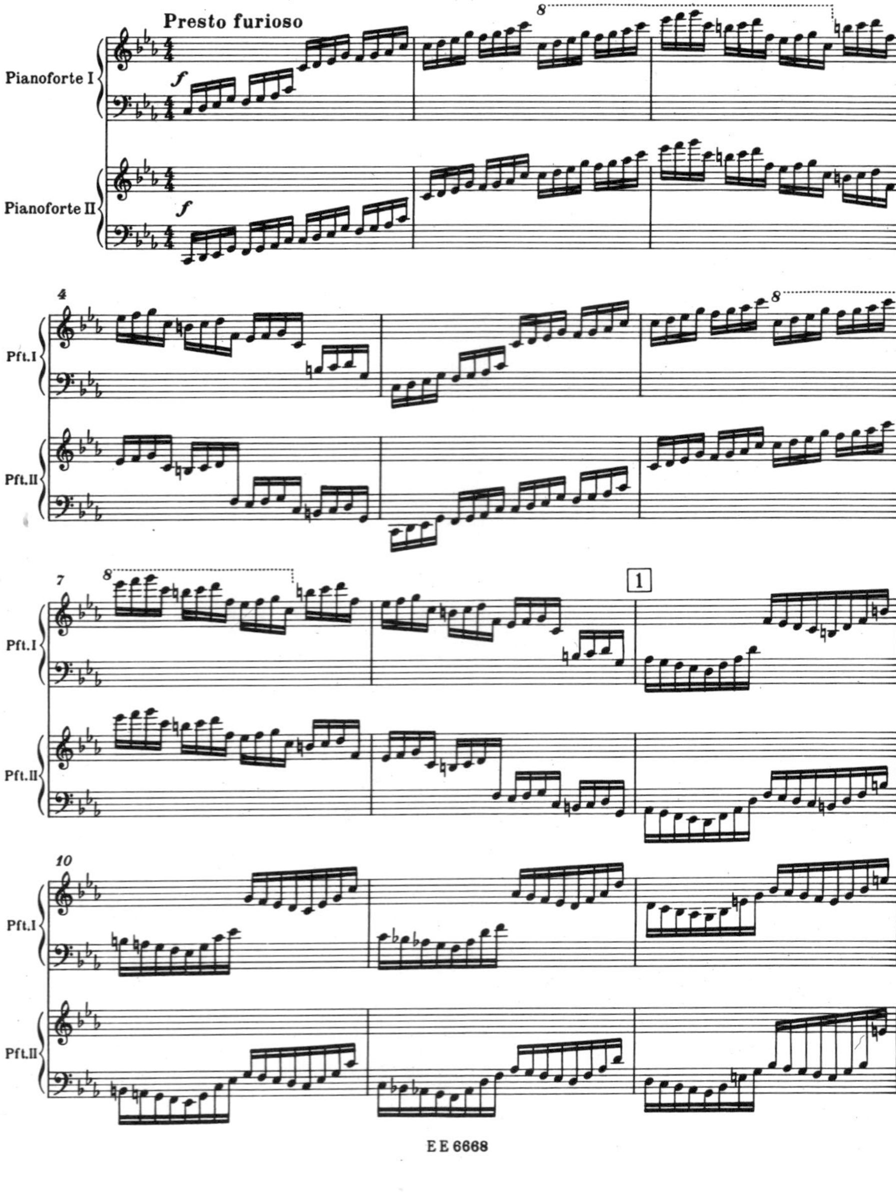

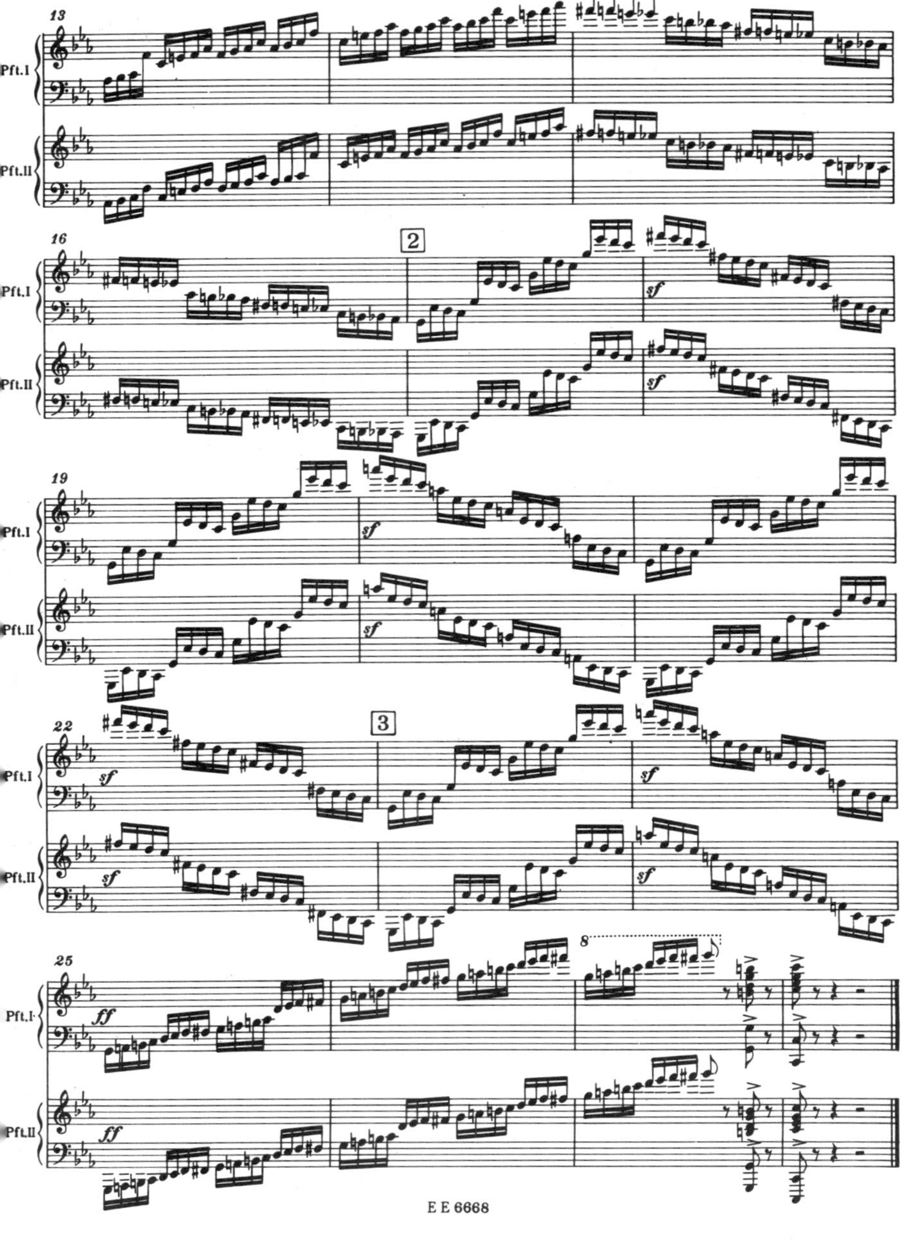
13
Pft.I
Pft.II
16
2
sf
19
sf
22
3
sf
25
ff
8

No.4 Tortues

Andante maestoso
Pianoforte I
pp
Violino I
Violino II
Viola
Violoncello
Contrabasso
pp
pp
pp
pp
pp
4
Pft.I
I
Vl.
II
Vla.
Vc.
Cb.

8
1
Pft.I
I
Vl.
II
Vla
Vc.
Cb.
12
Pft.I
I
Vl.
II
Vla.
Vc.
Cb.

2
Pft. I
I
Vl.
II
Vla.
Vc.
Cb.
rit.
Pft. I
I
Vl.
II
Vla.
Vc.
Cb.

No. 5 L'Éléphant

29
Pft.II
Cb.
35
3
f
41
4
ff
47

No. 6 Kangourous

No.7 Aquarium

4
Fl.
Arm.
[sim.]
Pft.I
sf
Pft.II
sf
I
Vl.
II
Vla.
Vc.
6
Fl.
Arm.
Pft.I
Pft.II
I
Vl.
II
Vla.
Vc.

8
1
Fl.
Arm.
Pft. I
Pft. II
I
Vl.
II
Vla.
Vc.
10
Fl.
Arm.
Pft. I
Pft. II
I
Vl.
II
Vla.
Vc.

13
Fl.
Arm.
Pft.I
Pft.II
I
Vl.
II
Vla.
Vc.
15
Fl.
Arm.
Pft.I
Pft.II
[sim.]
I
Vl.
II
Vla.
Vc.

17
2
Fl.
Arm.
Pft.I
Pft.II
I
Vl.
II
Vla.
Vc.
19
Fl.
Arm.
Pft.I
Pft.II
I
Vl.
II
Vla.
Vc.

21
Fl.
Arm.
Pft.I
Pft.II
I
Vl.
II
Vla.
Vc.
24
3
Fl.
Arm.
Pft.I
Pft.II
I
Vl.
II
Vla.
Vc.

26
Fl.
Arm.
Pft. I
Pft. II
I
Vl.
II
Vla.
Vc.
28
Fl.
Arm.
Pft. I
Pft. II
I
Vl.
II
Vla.
Vc.

31
4
Fl.
Arm.
Pft. I
Pft. II
Vl. I
Vl. II
Vla.
pizz.
Vc.
pizz.
33
Fl.
Arm.
Pft. I
Pft. II
Vl. I
Vl. II
Vla.
pizz.
Vc.
pizz.

35
Fl.
Arm.
Pft. I
Pft. II
I
Vl.
II
arco
Vla.
arco
Vc.
37
ppp
Ped.
Ped.
ôtez la Sourdine
ôtez la Sourdine
ôtez la Sourdine
ôtez la Sourdine

No. 8 Personnages à longues oreilles

No. 9 Le coucou au fond des bois

6
1
Cl. (B♭)
Pft.I
sempre pp
Pft.II
sempre pp
13
2
Cl. (B♭)
Pft.I
Pft.II
19
Cl. (B♭)
Pft.I
Ped.
Pft.II
Ped.

25
3
Cl. (B♭)
Pft. I
Pft. II
31
4
dim. sine al fine
pp
pp
37
8
ppp
ppp
ppp
Ped.
Ped.

No. 10

Volière

6
1
Fl.
I
Vl.
II
Vla.
Vc.
Cb.
9
Fl.
Pft.I
p
tr
Pft.II
p
tr
I
Vl.
II
Vla.
Vc.
Cb.

12
2
Fl.
Pft. I
Pft. II
I
Vl.
II
Vla.
Vc.
Cb.
15
Fl.
Pft. I
Pft. II
I
Vl.
II
Vla.
Vc.
Cb.

17
Fl.
Pft. I
Pft. II
Vl. I
Vl. II
Vla.
Vc.
Cb.
19
3

21
Fl.
Pft.I
Pft.II
Vl. I
Vl. II
Vla.
Vc.
Cb.
sul ponticello
sul ponticello
sul ponticello
arco
sul ponticello
pp
24
4

27
Fl.
Pft.I
Pft.II
I
Vl.
II
Vla.
Vc.
Cb.
29
pp
ppp
pizz.

No. 11 Pianistes

8
ft.I
ft.II
I
Vl.
II
Vla.
Vc.
Cb.
f
11
2

14
3
Pft. I
Pft. II
Vl.
I
II
Vla.
Vc.
Cb.
f
17

21
4
Pft. I
ff
Pft. II
ff
I
Vl.
II
Vla.
Vc.
Cb.
26
Pft. I
Pft. II
I
Vl.
II
Vla.
Vc.
Cb.

No. 12 Fossiles

11
Xil.
Pft.I
Pft.II
I
Vl.
II
Vla.
Vc.
Cb.
arco
pizz.
16
arco
pizz.

21
2
Xil.
Pft.I
Pft.II
p scherz.
I
Vl.
II
Vla.
Vc.
arco
Cb.
arco
26
Cl.
(B♭)
ff
Xil.
Pft.I
p scherz.
Pft.II
I
Vl.
II
p
p
Vla.
p
Vc.
p
Cb.
p

32
3
Cl. (B♭)
Xil.
Pft.I
Pft.II
I
Vl.
II
Vla.
Vc.
Cb.
ff
pizz.
37
8
arco

42
4
Cl. (B♭)
Xil.
Pft. I
Pft. II
Vl. I
Vl. II
Vla.
Vc.
Cb.
pizz.
arco
ff
8
47
p espress.
p

52
5
Cl. (B♭)
Xil.
Pft.I
Pft.II
Vl. I
Vl. II
Vla.
Vc.
Cb.
cresc.
pp
p
pizz.
58
f
brillante
arco

63
6
Cl. (B♭)
Xil.
Pft. I
Pft. II
I Vl. II
Vla.
Vc.
Cb.
ff
68
arco
8

No. 13

Le Cygne

5
Vc.
Pft.I
Pft.II
7
1
Vc.
Pft.I
Pft.II
9
Vc.
Pft.I
8
Pft.II

11
Vc.
Pft.I
8
Pft.II
13
15
2

17
Vc.
p
Pft.I
Pft.II
19
Vc.
Pft.I
Pft.II
21
3
Vc.
mf
Pft.I
Pft.II

23
Vc.
Pft.I
Pft.II
dim.
25
rit.
lento
a tempo
pp
pp
pp
8
27
rit.
pp

No. 14 Final

Molto allegro
Piccolo
Clarinetto (C)
Armonica
Xilofono
Pianoforte I
Pianoforte II
Violino I
Violino II
Viola
Violoncello
Contrabasso

Picc.
Cl. (C)
Arm.
Xil.
Pft. I
Pft. II
Vl. I
Vl. II
Vla.
Vc.
Cb.
tr
G
D
1
p
pizz.

16
2
tr
Picc.
Cl. (C)
Pft.I
Pft.II
p
Vc.
Cb.
21
cresc.

26
3
Picc.
Cl. (C)
Arm.
Xil.
Pft.I
Pft.II
Vl. I
Vl. II
Vla.
Vc.
Cb.
arco
29

32
8
Pft. I
Pft. II
I
Vl.
II
Vla.
Vc.
Cb.
35
4
Pft. I
Pft. II
I
Vl.
II
Vla.
Vc.
Cb.

38
Pft. I
Pft. II
I
Vl.
II
Vla.
Vc.
Cb.
41
8
Pft. I
Pft. II
I
Vl.
II
Vla.
Vc.
Cb.

44
5
Pft.I
Pft.II
I
Vl.
II
Vla.
Vc.
Cb.
pizz.
p
tr
49
6
Picc.
Cl.
(C)
Arm.
Xil.
8
f
arco

53
tr
Picc.
Cl.
(C)
Arm.
Xil.
8
Pft.I
Pft.II
I
Vl.
II
Vla.
Vc.
Cb.

57
Picc.
Cl. (C)
Arm.
Pft. I
Pft. II
Vl. I
Vl. II
Vla.
Vc.
Cb.

61
7
Picc.
Cl. (C)
Arm.
Pft. I
Pft. II
Vl. I
Vl. II
Vla.
Vc.
Cb.
66
Pft. I
Pft. II
Vl. I
Vl. II
Vla.
Vc.
Cb.

71
8
Pft. I
cresc.
Pft. II
cresc.
I
Vl.
II
p cresc.
p
cresc.
Vla.
cresc.
Vc.
cresc.
Cb.
cresc.
75
Pft. I
f
Pft. II
f
I
Vl.
II
f
Vla.
f
Vc.
f
Cb.
f

77
9
Picc.
Cl. (C)
Arm.
Xil.
Pft.I
Pft.II
I
Vl.
II
Vla.
Vc.
Cb.
f
8

80
Picc.
Cl. (C)
Arm.
Xil.
8
Pft. I
Pft. II
I
Vl.
II
Vla.
Vc.
Cb.

83
10
Picc.
Cl. (C)
Arm.
Xil.
Pft. I
Pft. II
Vl. I
Vl. II
Vla.
Vc.
Cb.

87
Picc.
Cl. (C)
Arm.
Xil.
Pft. I
Pft. II
I
Vl.
II
Vla.
Vc.
Cb.
ff
8